W9-BCY-078

Science STARTS

GEARS GO! WHEELS ROLL!

by Mark Weakland

CAPSTONE PRESS
a capstone imprint

Wheels are all around us. At the fair a Ferris wheel spins gracefully in the night. While unseen wheels turn inside clocks and computers, most others are easy to spot.

Wheels come in all sizes. Small wheels roll under rollerblades, scooters, and skateboards.

4

Buses, race cars, and semitrucks rumble along on big wheels.

Tractors roll through fields on big and small wheels. Tractor tires fit perfectly between rows of crops so plants won't get crushed.

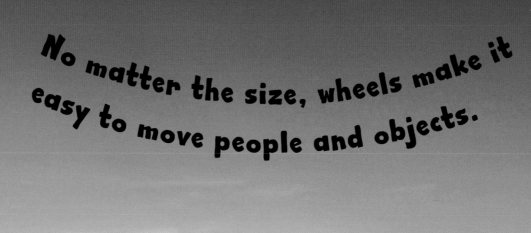

No matter the size, wheels make it easy to move people and objects.

Without wheels you would have to drag that wagon or carry heavy weights. Why work so hard?

We use wheels to travel quickly and easily. Buses, cabs, subways, and trains use wheels. Airplanes use them when leaving and landing.

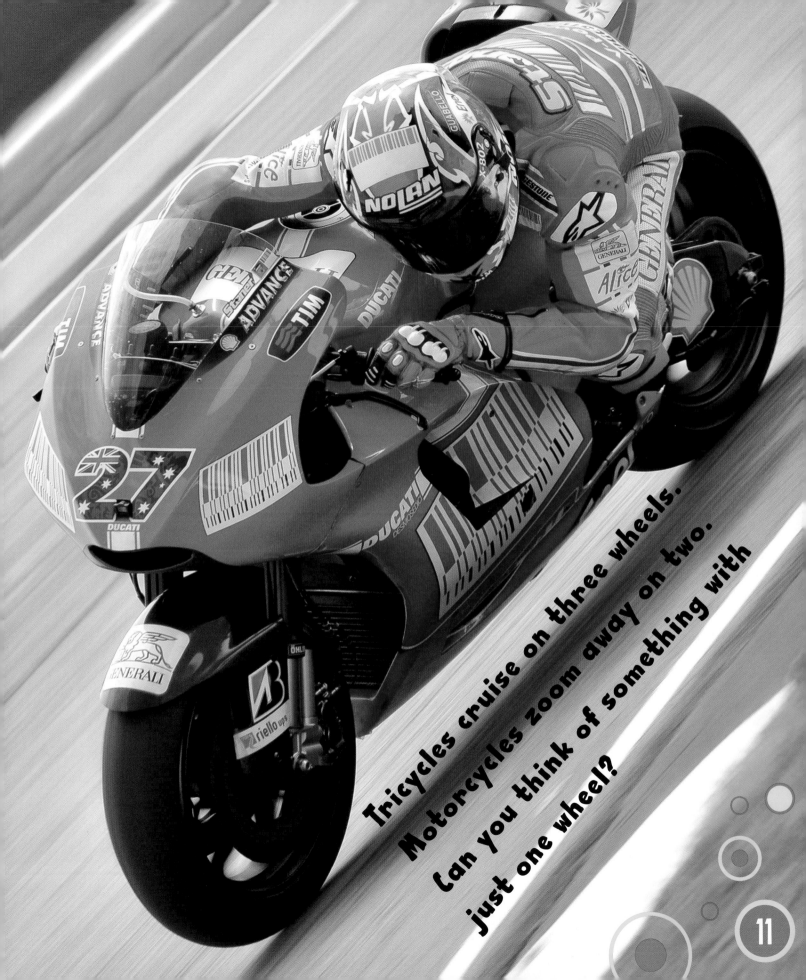

Tricycles cruise on three wheels.
Motorcycles zoom away on two.
Can you think of something with
just one wheel?

On a wheelbarrow, one wheel turns around one axle.

axle

12

Axles hold wheels in place
while allowing them to turn.
For wheels to work, they
need an axle.

Doorknobs act like two wheels. Connected by an axle in the door, turning a doorknob moves the latch.

Turn the knob, and you're turning a wheel!

There are many wheels and axles on a car.

Two front wheels turn around one axle. Two back wheels use another.

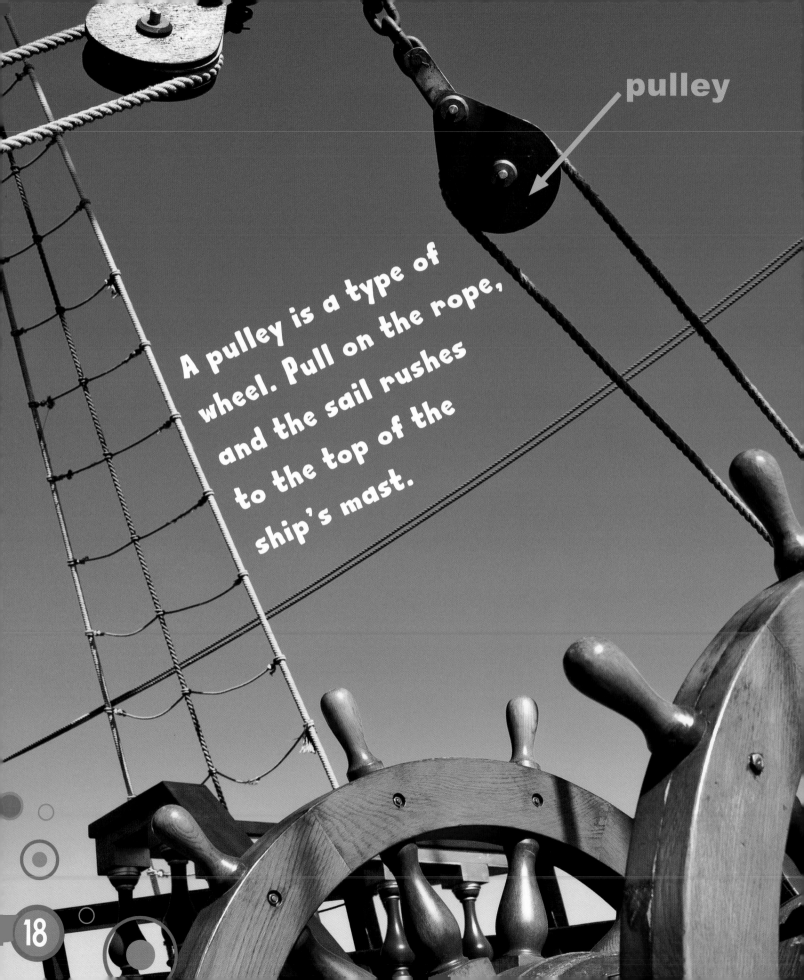

pulley

A pulley is a type of wheel. Pull on the rope, and the sail rushes to the top of the ship's mast.

On a crane many pulleys work together. With pulleys and cables, a crane can lift lots of metal.

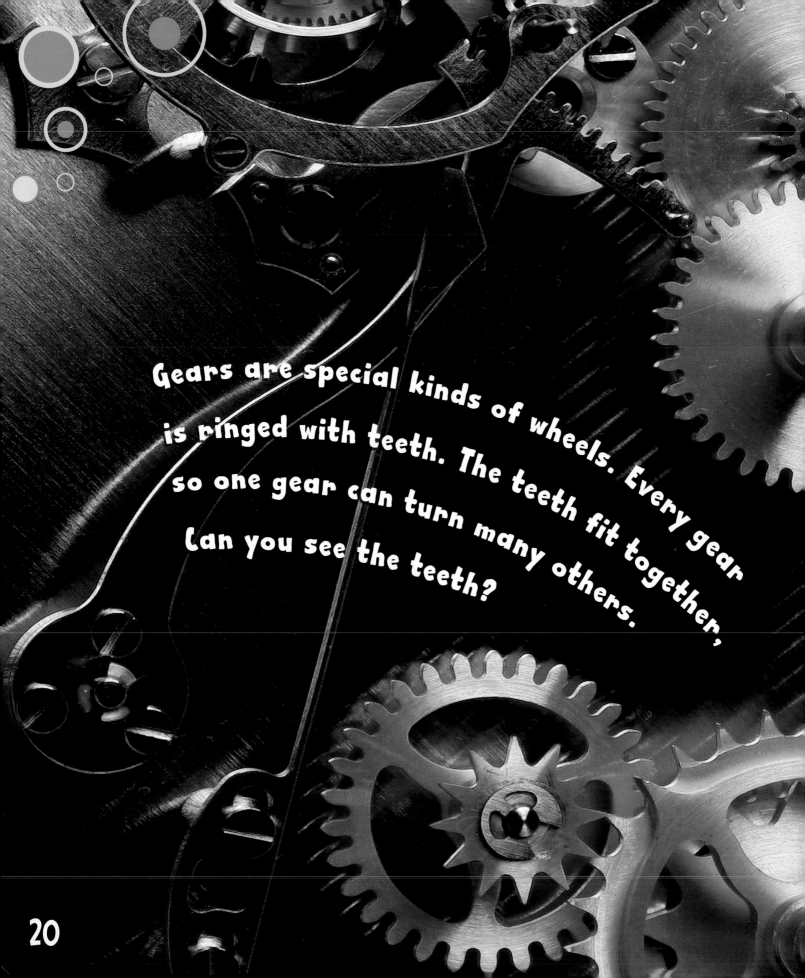

Gears are special kinds of wheels. Every gear is ringed with teeth. The teeth fit together, so one gear can turn many others. Can you see the teeth?

20

Gears send power from one place to another. Gears connected to a motor move a robot's arms and legs.

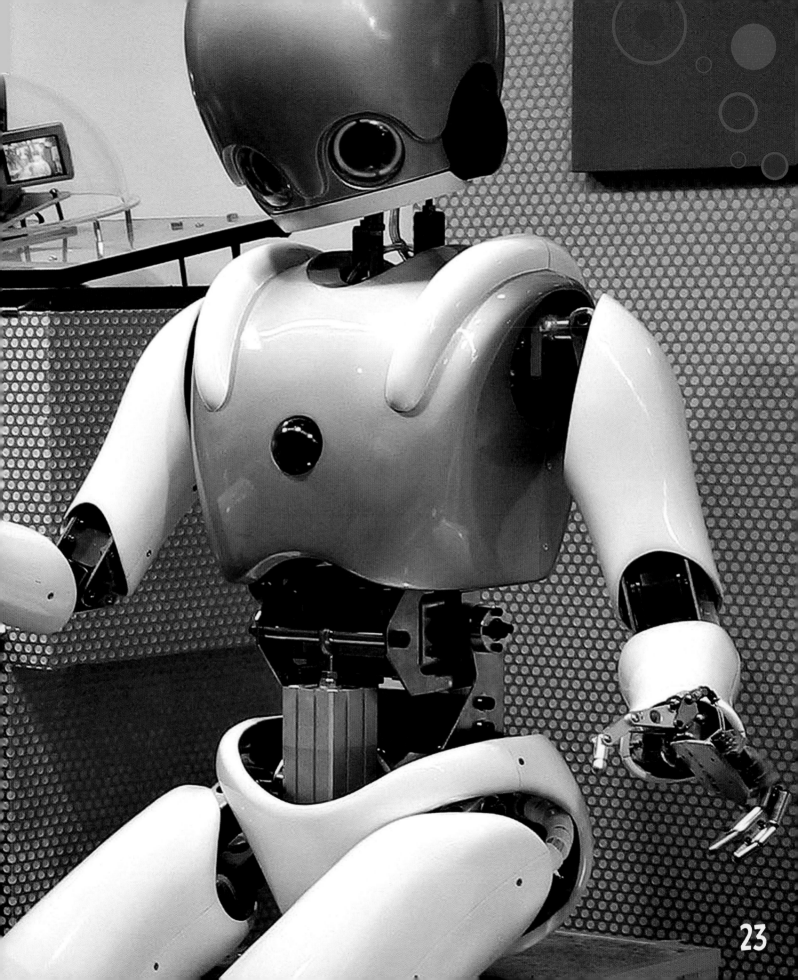

Bicycles have gears with large teeth. The front gears are linked to the back gears by a bike chain.

Gears, a chain, and strong legs power a bike's back wheel.

Watches and clocks with hands contain many gears. Tiny gears quietly whirr and buzz, spinning round and round. The gears turn the second hand, minute hand, and hour hand.

Wheels and gears are busy
doing work all around us.

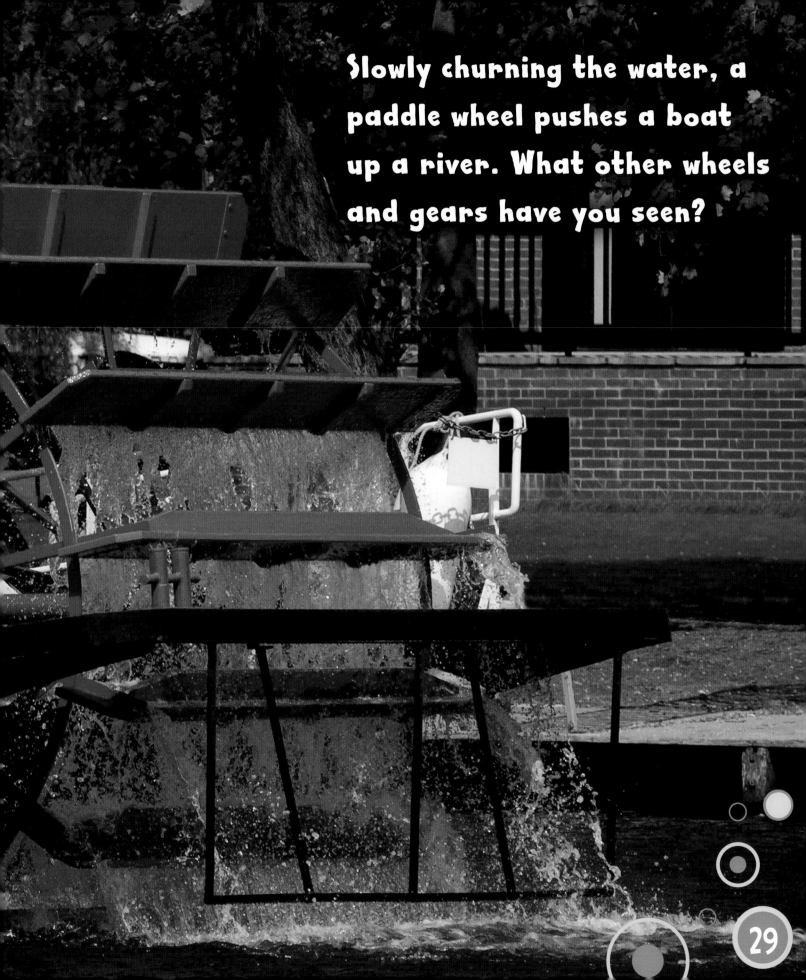

Slowly churning the water, a paddle wheel pushes a boat up a river. What other wheels and gears have you seen?

Glossary

axle—a bar in the center of a wheel around which a wheel turns

cable—a thick wire

crane—a machine with a long arm used to lift and move heavy objects

gear—a toothed wheel that fits into another toothed wheel

pulley—a rope around a wheel with a grooved rim; a pulley makes it easier to lift or move objects

Read MORE

Challen, Paul. *Get to Know Wheels and Axles*. Get to Know Simple Machines. New York: Crabtree Pub. Company, 2009.

Glover, David. *Pulleys and Gears*. Simple Machines. Chicago: Heinemann Library, 2006.

Prince, April Jones. *What Do Wheels Do All Day?* Boston: Houghton Mifflin, 2006.

Internet SITES

FactHound offers a safe, fun way to find Internet sites related to this book. All of the sites on FactHound have been researched by our staff.

Here's all you do:

Visit *www.facthound.com*

Type in this code: 9781429652537

Check out projects, games and lots more at
www.capstonekids.com

Index

A+ Books are published by
Capstone Press,
151 Good Counsel Drive, P.O. Box 669,
Mankato, Minnesota 56002.
www.capstonepub.com

Books published by Capstone Press are manufactured with paper
containing at least 10 percent post-consumer waste.

Library of Congress Cataloging-in-Publication Data
Weakland, Mark.
  Gears go, wheels roll / by Mark Weakland.
    p. cm.—(A+ books. Science starts)
  Summary: "Simple text and photographs explain the basic science behind wheels and gears"—Provided
  by publisher.
    Includes bibliographical references and index.
      ISBN 978-1-4296-5253-7 (lib. bdg.) — ISBN 978-1-4296-6143-0 (pbk.)
        1. Gearing—Juvenile literature. 2. Wheels—Juvenile literature. I. Title. II. Series.
        TJ181.5.W43 2011
        621.8'33—dc22   2010038880

Credits

Jenny Marks, editor; Alison Thiele, designer; Marcie Spence, media researcher; Eric Manske, production specialist

Photo Credits

Capstone Studio: Karon Dubke, cover; iStockphoto: silverlining56, 14–15, ssj414, 8–9, Ugurbarskan, 19; Shutterstock: afaizal,
11, Alexander V Evstafyev, 20–21, Anyka, 26–27, Christian Lagerek, 5, DeshaCAM, 6–7, Galina Barskaya, 4, GWImages, 1, Jamie
Robinson, 12–13, jordache, 2–3, Maridav, 24–25, Mikael Damkier, 16–17, pandapaw, 18, Steve Mann, 28–29, Supertrooper, 10,
Theodore Littleton, 22–23.

Note to Parents, Teachers, and Librarians

The Science Starts series supports national education standards related to science. This book describes and illustrates gears and wheels.
The images support early readers in understanding the text. The repetition of words and phrases helps early readers learn new words.
This book also introduces early readers to subject-specific vocabulary words, which are defined in the Glossary section. Early readers
may need assistance to read some words and to use the Glossary, Read More, Internet Sites, and Index sections of the book.

Printed in the United States of America
in North Mankato, Minnesota.
092010   005933CGS11